Cook, Pot, Cook!

Written by David Bedford

Illustrated by Jimothy Rolovio

OXFORD

UNIVERSITY PRESS

Tess got a pot.

4

The pot was boiling.

Look at all the food, Mum!

7

That night ...

The pot was full!
It did not stop!

Look at all the
food, Mum!

The food got to Nan in her chair.

Look at all the food, Nan!

Stop, pot, stop!

The food took Nan down the road.

13

The town was a mess!

Look at all this mess, Nan!

Once upon a time...

The end.